D1522954

Animal Attacks

MOUNTAIN LION ATTACK

by Lisa Owings

BELLWETHER MEDIA · MINNEAPOLIS, MN

Are you ready to take it to the extreme?
Torque books thrust you into the action-
packed world of sports, vehicles, mystery,
and adventure. These books may include
dirt, smoke, fire, and dangerous stunts.
WARNING: read at your own risk.

Library of Congress Cataloging-in-Publication Data

Owings, Lisa.
 Mountain lion attack / by Lisa Owings.
   p. cm. -- (Torque: animal attacks)
 Includes bibliographical references and index.
 Summary: "Engaging images illustrate true mountain lion attack stories and accompany survival tips.
The combination of high-interest subject matter and light text is intended for students in grades 3
through 7"--Provided by publisher.
 ISBN 978-1-60014-789-0 (hardcover : alk. paper)
 ISBN 978-1-60014-845-3 (paperback : alk. paper)
 1. Puma attacks--Juvenile literature. 2. Puma--Behavior--Juvenile literature. I. Title.
QL737.C23O956 2013
599.75'24--dc23

                                                2012011224

This edition first published in 2013 by Bellwether Media, Inc.

Printed in the United States of America, North Mankato, MN.

A special thanks to Brian Smale for contributing an image.

TABLE OF CONTENTS

Night Stalker

The mountain lion is a fearsome **wild cat**. It **stalks** its **prey** under the cover of night. Then it leaps on top of its **victim**. Its powerful jaws easily snap the prey's neck. Its sharp teeth crunch through the spine. The mountain lion will feast on the **carcass** for days. You do not want to become its next meal!

Buried Treasure

A mountain lion buries its kill under dirt or leaves. This hides the food from animals that might steal it. The mountain lion comes back again and again to feed.

5

Trail of Death

Mountain biker Anne Hjelle raced down a rugged California trail. Her friend Debi Nicholls was close behind. Anne whizzed around curves and past a deserted bike. She had no idea she was being hunted. Suddenly Anne saw a flash of reddish fur. Then a mountain lion slammed her to the ground.

What Anne Didn't Know
The deserted bike belonged to
Mark Reynolds. The mountain lion
had killed him just hours before it
attacked Anne.

The cat's jaws closed on the back of Anne's neck. She let out a chilling scream as it dragged her toward the bushes. Debi jumped off her bike and threw it at the mountain lion. She grabbed Anne's leg and held on tight. Soon the mountain lion let go of Anne's neck. But only to sink its teeth into her face.

"I remember thinking, This is it. I'm going to die."

—Anne Hjelle

The Unlucky Few

Mountain lions attack about six people in North America every year.

8

Anne could feel her flesh rip away. Then the wild cat **lunged** for her throat. Its teeth pierced deep into the skin. Anne struggled to breathe. She passed out as blood flowed from her neck.

Other bikers had heard the women's screams. They threw stones at the animal. Finally a stone hit the cat in the head and it ran off. One biker called 911. Soon Anne was on her way to the hospital. Today, Anne's scars are reminders of her fight for survival.

"The left side of my face was peeled away to my nose in one big slab of meat."

—Anne Hjelle

A Fresh Face

Doctors operated on Anne for more than five hours. It took 200 stitches and several more surgeries to repair her face.

Anne Hjelle

Guardian Angel

Eleven-year-old Austin Forman
was gathering firewood in his
backyard in southwestern Canada.
It was dark except for the glow of
house lights. Austin's golden retriever,
Angel, seemed nervous. Austin soon
found out why. A killer mountain
lion sprang out of the woods and ran
straight for him.

"The dog knew something was up because she ran toward me just at the right time."

—Austin Forman

Angel leaped over a lawn mower to get between the mountain lion and Austin. The wild cat brutally attacked the dog. Austin ran inside for help. "There's a cougar eating Angel!" he screamed. He could hear Angel **yelping** in pain. The cougar was killing the dog that had just saved his life.

Fierce by Any Name

Mountain lions are also called puma, cougars, panthers, and catamounts.

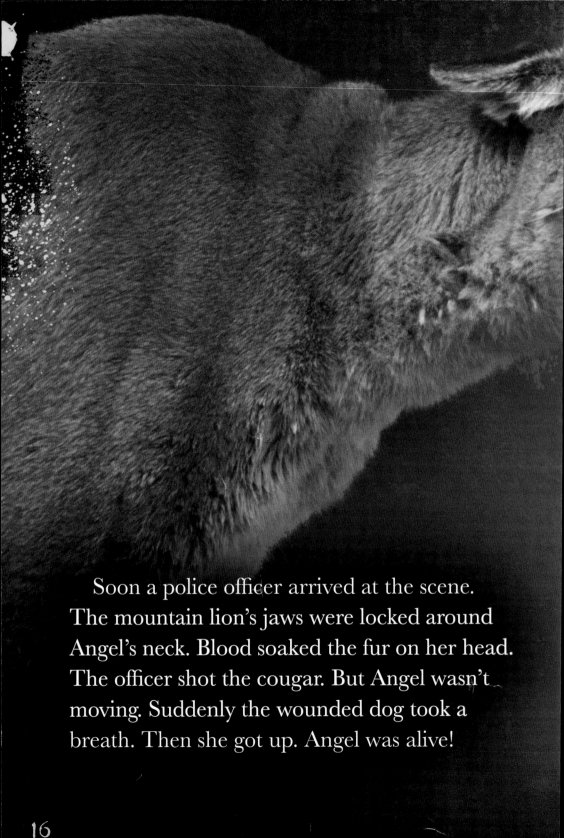

Soon a police officer arrived at the scene. The mountain lion's jaws were locked around Angel's neck. Blood soaked the fur on her head. The officer shot the cougar. But Angel wasn't moving. Suddenly the wounded dog took a breath. Then she got up. Angel was alive!

Best Friends

Angel limped over to Austin right after the attack. She checked to make sure he was okay. Austin later bought Angel a juicy steak as a thank-you for saving his life.

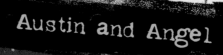

Austin and Angel

Prevent a Mountain Lion Attack

Mountain lions are most likely to attack children or lone adults. To prevent an attack, travel with a group when in mountain lion **territory**. Keep an eye out for mountain lion tracks and fresh kills. Do not enter mountain lion territory at night. This is when they are on the prowl. If you see a mountain lion nearby, back away from it slowly.

Leaps and Bounds

Mountain lions can jump up to 18 feet (5.5 meters) high. They can also travel 40 feet (12 meters) in a single leap.

Survive a Mountain Lion Attack

Do not run or turn away if you come face-to-face with a mountain lion. Make yourself look as large and scary as possible. Stand tall, raise your arms, and speak loudly. If the mountain lion attacks, fight for your life. Hit it hard in the face. A few minutes of being brave could save you from a **fatal** bite.

More Survival Tips

- **DO** defend yourself with whatever is nearby. Hit the mountain lion with sticks and rocks.

- **DO** stay on your feet during the attack. You risk a fatal bite if you play dead.

- **DON'T** bend down to grab sticks or rocks if a mountain lion is very close.

- **DON'T** give up. Mountain lions prefer easy prey. They won't put up with a fight for long.

Glossary

carcass—a dead body

fatal—resulting in death

lunged—rushed forward suddenly

prey—an animal that is hunted by another animal for food

stalks—hunts or tracks prey in a quiet, secret way

territory—the area of land where an animal lives, searches for food, and raises its young

victim—a person or animal that is hurt, killed, or made to suffer

wild cat—one of several types of cats that live in the wild; bobcats, lynx, and mountain lions are wild cats.

yelping—crying out sharply

To Learn More

AT THE LIBRARY

Long, Denise. *Survivor Kid: A Practical Guide to Wilderness Survival*. Chicago, Ill.: Chicago Review Press, 2011.

Markle, Sandra. *Mountain Lions*. Minneapolis, Minn.: Lerner Publications Company, 2010.

Read, Tracy C. *Exploring the World of Cougars*. Richmond Hill, Ont.: Firefly Books, 2011.

ON THE WEB

Learning more about

mountain lions is as easy as 1, 2, 3.

1. Go to www.factsurfer.com.

2. Enter "mountain lions" into the search box.

3. Click the "Surf" button and you will see a list of related Web sites.

With factsurfer.com, finding more information is just a click away.

Index